Read! Write! Publish!

Making Books in the Classroom

Grades 1–5

Written by Barbara Fairfax and Adela Garcia

Illustrated by Terri Rae

Edited by Janet Bruno

CTP © 1992, Creative Teaching Press, Inc., Cypress, CA 90630

One successful way to stimulate an interest in writing and foster a lifelong love of reading is to involve students in making their own books. Children love to read what they have written and take considerable pride in their published work. Student-authored books are among the most popular books in any classroom library.

Celebrating authorship by publishing books is also an important component of the writing process. It gives students a real reason to move writing through the whole authoring cycle: prewriting, drafting, revising, editing, and publishing. Writing for an audience provides an opportunity to practice writing skills in a meaningful way.

Read! Write! Publish! makes it easy for you to publish student work. In the pages that follow you will find:

- Step-by-step directions for making 20 different books
- A complete list of materials needed for each book
- 120 cross-curricular writing ideas for students of all grade levels
- Suggested literature selections to use as models for writing
- Ideas for individual and class books
- A complete bibliography for all titles mentioned
- Reproducible patterns and forms

Read! Write! Publish!

Table of Contents

Tips on Using This Book

Students of all ages can participate successfully in making books. Consider the following options when using the writing and publishing activities in *Read! Write! Publish!*

✍ Students write, illustrate, and publish their own individual books.

✍ Each child does one page for a class book.

✍ Cooperative learning groups collaborate on writing and illustrating a book.

✍ A student author writes a story and "hires" another student to illustrate it.

✍ An older student and a younger child write and illustrate a book together.

Peek-over Book

Barney, the Bashful Bear
by Casey B.

Materials
* reproducible page 55
* (copied on construction paper)
  scissors
* crayons, markers
* scraps of colored paper
* 4-1/2" x 8" writing paper
* stapler

Instructions for Making the Book

1. Use crayons, markers, or paper scraps to make an animal at the top of the peek-over cover.

2. Cut on solid lines only. You will have to poke your scissors through the paper to cut under the paws and chin.

3. Staple sheets of writing paper to the bottom portion.

4. Fold up on the fold line so the bottom portion tucks under the paws and chin.

5. Write the title of the book on the front.

Bear Facts
by Judy

10   *Read! Write! Publish!*   Creative Teaching Press

Direction Pages

The direction pages give you step-by-step instructions for making the books. You will also find a complete list of materials needed for each student. In most cases, the size of each book and the types of materials used can be changed to fit your needs.

When student stories have been revised and edited and are ready to be published, follow the steps below:

1. Read over the directions and prepare a sample book.

2. Gather all necessary materials and supplies. Some books will require you to reproduce a page for each student. All reproducibles are at the back of this book. Most of these pages can be duplicated on regular copier paper or on construction paper.

3. **Model book assembly for students, carefully demonstrating and explaining each step.** You may want to reproduce copies of the direction page to give to students.

4. Assemble covers as a class project or set up a book publishing center for use by small groups.

Writing Idea Pages

Each book cover has a companion page of nongraded cross-curricular writing ideas that children of all ages and abilities will enjoy. Since the core of any language arts program is quality literature, writing ideas for specific picture books and chapter books are included. Use the annotated descriptions of these books to help you choose appropriate writing activities for your students. In most cases, however, you can substitute any book with a similar theme. You will find a bibliography listing all titles, authors, and publishers on pages 69–70.

If you are an upper grade teacher, don't hesitate to use the suggested picture book titles. Picture books make an exciting lesson possible in a limited amount of time. They contain all the elements of good writing and are an effective tool in developing difficult concepts. The wonderful illustrations and rich language of picture books appeal to children of all ages.

After participating in several bookmaking activities, you will find that your students will come up with their own meaningful writing topics and innovative book covers. Use the Bright Idea Brainstorming reproducible on page 52 to aid students in the prewriting stage when they are generating and organizing writing ideas. Other techniques helpful at this stage are webbing, clustering, making lists and word banks, discussing, and role-playing.

Writing Ideas for Peek-over Book

What Do You See?
Students write their own stories following the pattern from the book *Brown Bear, Brown Bear, What Do You See?* by Bill Martin, Jr.

Example
"Spotted toad, spotted toad, what do you see?"
"I see a dragonfly looking at me."

"Spotted toad, Spotted toad, what do you see?" "I see a dragonfly looking at me."

Stuffed Animals
In *Ira Sleeps Over* by Bernard Waber a young boy must decide whether to take his reassuring teddy bear when he spends the night with a friend. Students make a Peek-over Book that looks like their favorite stuffed animal and then write about the animal.

Rotten Adventures
Children delight in the mischievous antics of Sarah's cat in *Rotten Ralph* by Jack Gantos. They will enjoy writing additional rotten adventures about Ralph.

Descriptive Language
Have students write a story about a real or an imaginary animal. Encourage the use of descriptive words that call upon the five senses: touch, sight, hearing, smell, and taste.

Animal Book Review
After reading a book in which an animal is an important character, students write a review of or a report about the book. Suggested titles: *Doctor De Soto* by William Steig, *Corduroy* by Don Freeman, *Millions of Cats* by Wanda Gag, the *Frog and Toad* series by Arnold Lobel, *Where the Red Fern Grows* by Wilson Rawls, *The Story of Jumping Mouse* by John Steptoe.

Dr. De Soto

Title
Older students will enjoy creating animal science books for younger children. Students select an animal to research and write scientific facts about it.

What I Know About Tigers by Sandy

Creative Teaching Press   *Read! Write! Publish!*   11

Magic Castle

Under the Sea

The big brown bear swung his paw down by the beehive.

Materials and Techniques for Making Books

Although specific directions and materials are listed for each book, you may want to vary the covers and page illustrations by using some of the materials and techniques listed below.

Cover Materials

- ☐ cardboard
- ☐ index board
- ☐ posterboard
- ☐ tagboard
- ☐ railroad board
- ☐ construction paper
- ☐ manila folders
- ☐ thin wood
- ☐ wallpaper
- ☐ bags (brown or decorative)
- ☐ fabric
- ☐ contact paper
- ☐ classified ads or comics
- ☐ butcher paper

Art Techniques to Use on Covers or Page Illustrations

- ↝ tissue paper collage
- ↝ printing designs
- ↝ straw-blown designs
- ↝ thumbprint art
- ↝ finger paintings
- ↝ crayon-resist drawings
- ↝ sponge painting
- ↝ string painting
- ↝ potato prints
- ↝ stencils
- ↝ rubbings
- ↝ photographs
- ↝ magazine pictures
- ↝ border drawings
- ↝ material scraps

Tran's kite soared above the clouds.

Room 7's Best Jokes

Kevin was lost in a dense jungle

Mittens loves to sleep on top of a warm TV.

Life Under the Sea

Adela's Poems

Me, age 6 months at Grandma Kraemer's.

Read! Write! Publish!

Ways to Bind Books

1. Staple

2. Sew
- machine-stitched
- hand-stitched with crewel needles and embroidery thread

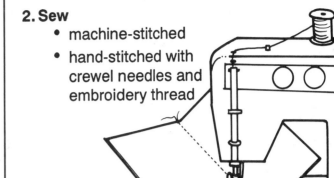

3. Punch holes and use:

paper fasteners

rings (shower curtain, key chain, notebook)

yarn

ribbon

twine or string

chicken bands/Chinese jacks

shoelaces

4. Plastic spiral binding (requires a machine)

Refining Your Books

To give books a finished professional look, consider adding some or all of the following touches:

Title Page and Publishing Information

Have students make a title page featuring the book's title, author, illustrator, and publisher. The class will enjoy inventing a publishing company name such as Brontosaurus Book Company or Sunshine Writers, Inc. Using the correct copyright format, students put the copyright information on the back of the title page.

Dedication Page (reproducible page 53)

Students select someone for the book dedication and think of the reason this person is special to them. This information is written on the dedication form and glued to the page following the title page.

Meet the Author (reproducible page 53)

Students fill in autobiographical information on the author form and glue it on the back cover. A small photo can be added to this page. Use photocopies of school pictures for this purpose.

Illustrations

Encourage children to add colorful borders to their text and to illustrate pages where appropriate. A variety of art media can be used for illustrations.

Library Pocket and Card

Students make a library pocket with a card so that books can be checked out and shared with family, friends, school personnel, and so on. Write the title and the author of the book at the top of a 3" x 5" index card. Cut a letter-size envelope in half. Glue the flap shut and glue the envelope seam side down inside the front cover.

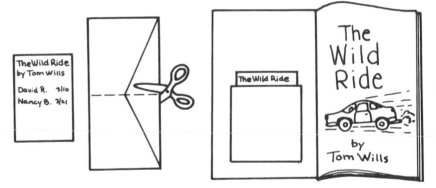

Readers' Comment Sheet (reproducible page 54)

Send the Readers' Comment Sheet home with the child so parents can write a comment about the book. Students can take home books written by classmates and solicit comments from family members, relatives, neighbors, and others. Reading these wonderful comments is very motivating for young authors! The Readers' Comment Sheet can be kept in an envelope glued to a final blank page in the book.

Readers' Comments

Jimmy has written a terrific book — I really enjoyed it. I particularly liked the very colorful dinosaur illustrations. Great job!

Mrs. James

Peek-over Book

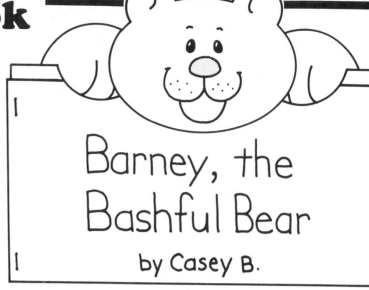

Barney, the Bashful Bear

by Casey B.

Materials

- reproducible page 55 (copied on construction paper)
- scissors
- crayons, markers
- scraps of colored paper
- 4" x 8" writing paper
- stapler

Instructions for Making the Book

1. Use crayons, markers, or paper scraps to make an animal at the top of the peek-over cover.

2. Cut on the solid lines only. You will have to poke your scissors through the paper to cut under the paws and chin.

3. Staple sheets of writing paper to the bottom portion.

4. Fold up on the fold line so the bottom portion tucks under the paws and chin.

5. Write the title of the book on the front.

Bear Facts

by Judy

Writing Ideas for Peek-over Book

What Do You See?

Students write their own stories following the pattern from the book *Brown Bear, Brown Bear, What Do You See?* by Bill Martin, Jr.

Example:
"Spotted toad, spotted toad, what do you see?"
"I see a dragonfly looking at me."

Stuffed Animals

In *Ira Sleeps Over* by Bernard Waber a young boy must decide whether to take his reassuring teddy bear when he spends the night with a friend. Students make a Peek-over Book that looks like their favorite stuffed animal and then write about the animal.

Rotten Adventures

Children delight in the mischievous antics of Sarah's cat in *Rotten Ralph* by Jack Gantos. They will enjoy writing additional Rotten Ralph adventures.

Descriptive Language

Have students write a story about a real or an imaginary animal. Encourage the use of descriptive words that appeal to the five senses: touch, sight, hearing, smell, and taste.

Animal Book Review

After reading a book in which an animal is an important character, students write a review of or a report about the book. Suggested titles: *Doctor De Soto* by William Steig, *Corduroy* by Don Freeman, *Millions of Cats* by Wanda Gag, the *Frog and Toad* series by Arnold Lobel, *Where the Red Fern Grows* by Wilson Rawls, *The Story of Jumping Mouse* by John Steptoe.

Scientific Facts

Older students will enjoy creating animal science books for younger children. Students select an animal to research and write scientific facts about it.

Envelope Book

Materials

- reproducible page 56
- scissors
- glue
- crayons, markers
- 2 pieces of 6" x 9" heavy paper for cover
- stapler

Instructions for Making the Book

1. Cut the envelope reproducible page on the heavy solid line. (Students will need one reproducible page 56 for each page of their book.)

2. Fold the page in half and glue the side edges to form an envelope. Be sure to keep the glue close to the edges.

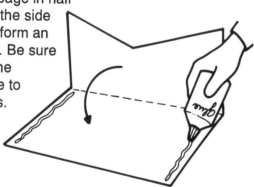

3. Write a letter, card, invitation, or announcement and put it inside the envelope.

4. Address the envelope. Design a stamp and make a postmark.

5. To form a book, place several envelopes between two 6" x 9" cover sheets. Staple on the left side and write a title on the front cover.

6. Variation: Use real envelopes with the flaps cut off and spiral bind them into a book.

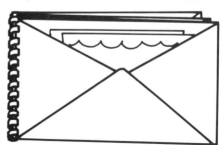

Writing Ideas for Envelope Book

Thank You, Santa

The Polar Express by Chris Van Allsburg tells of a young boy's Christmas Eve adventure at the North Pole. Students write thank-you letters to Mr. Claus for the wonderful trip aboard the Polar Express.

Party Invitation

Students write invitations to a unique party; for example, a Kite Flying Party at the park or a Funny Hat Party.

AROUND THE WORLD PARTY
APRIL 28
2:00 to 5:00
Wear a foreign costume.

Fairy Tale Mail

The Jolly Postman by Janet and Allan Ahlberg is a humorous collection of correspondence sent to fairy tale characters. Students write a letter, thank-you note, invitation, or announcement from one fairy tale character to another.

Dear Bear Family,
I'm sorry I broke baby bear's chair.

Goldilocks

Wish You Were Here

After reading *Stringbean's Trip to the Shining Sea* by Vera Williams, students pretend they are on a trip and write letters to friends or relatives. The destination can be real or imaginary.

Dear Mario,
You should see the view from the top of the Eiffel Tower!
Love,
Raquel

Mario Siquiera
Curitiba, Brazil
S.A.

Dear Mr. President

Students write letters to the President asking questions about his job, telling what they would do if they were president, or describing what they would like to see improved or changed. Copies of the letters can be used for a class book and the originals can be sent to the President.

Dear Mr. President,
Please spend more money to save endangered animals.
Very Truly yours,
Richard

Life on the Trail

Students pretend they are traveling west in a wagon train like the main character in *Cassie's Journey: Going West in the 1860s* by Brett Harvey. Then they write a letter to a friend or relative describing life on the trail.

Pop-up Book

Materials

- reproducible page 57
- scissors
- drawing paper
- crayons, markers
- 12" x 18" heavy paper for cover
- glue

Instructions for Making the Book

1. Fold reproducible page 57 in half and cut along the solid tab lines. Refold so that the writing lines are on the inside. Close the page and press firmly.

2. Open the page and push the tabs to the inside.

3. On another piece of paper draw the objects you want to pop up. Cut them out and glue them to the tabs as shown. Make sure the picture does not extend below the tab.

4. Write a story on the lines provided.

5. To assemble the book, glue the completed pages together as shown.

6. Use one large sheet of heavy paper or tagboard to make a cover as shown. Glue it to the front and back pages of the book.

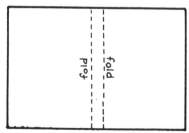

Writing Ideas for Pop-up Book

Animal Rhyme

After reading the humorous updated version of *Chicken Little* by Steven Kellogg, students create a rhyming name for an animal; for example, Snakey Lakey. Then they write an adventure for that animal and illustrate it.

Shoes

Students read or listen to a book about shoes, such as *Alligator Shoes* by Arthur Dorros or *Shoes* by Elizabeth Winthrop. Then they draw or cut out pictures of shoes and write couplets about different types of shoes.

Example:
High-top shoes are really cool,
But never wear them in the pool.

History Pop-up

Create a Pop-up Book of specialized vocabulary for science or history.

Egyptian History

Pharaoh – a king of ancient Egypt.

Sphinx – mythical creature with the body of a lion and the head of a man.

Collective Nouns

Have students make a class book about collective nouns patterned after *A Cache of Jewels*, a beautifully illustrated rhyming book by Ruth Heller. To make the activity more challenging, they can brainstorm alliterative phrases using collective nouns.

A bunch of busy boys.

Famous People

Make a class book of famous people. Each student picks a different person to research and summarizes the person's claim to fame on one page of the Pop-up Book.

Ben Franklin was a famous American statesman. Did you know that he invented bifocals?

Fun With Vocabulary

In *Q Is for Duck* by Mary Elting and Michael Folsom students are challenged to figure out why "*A* is for zoo" and "*C* is for hen." Using the pattern in the book, students illustrate vocabulary words and write an explanation on the lines.

Examples:
S is for viper because a viper is a snake.

M is for ruler because a ruler is used for measuring.

Shirt Book

Materials

- 12" x 18" construction paper
- ruler/pencil
- scissors
- glue
- 8-1/2" x 11" writing paper
- stapler
- wallpaper scraps, fabric scraps, buttons, ribbons, trims

Instructions for Making the Book

1. Fold a piece of 12" x 18" construction paper in half widthwise.

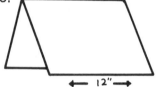

2. Measure down about 2" from the folded edge and, keeping the paper folded, cut in 3" on each side.

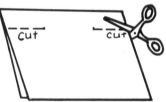

3. Fold each cut piece inward diagonally to form a collar. Glue down.

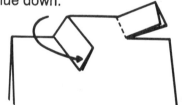

4. Staple the completed story to the inside of the shirt.

5. Decorate the shirt with buttons and a pocket made of wallpaper or fabric. Add a tie for a man or a bow for a woman. Add other details to make the shirt match the story.

6. Write the title of the book and the author's name on the side opposite the pocket.

Writing Ideas for Shirt Book

Clothes Time

Each student uses his/her own name, picks a color and an article of clothing, and writes a sentence following the pattern in the book *Mary Wore Her Red Dress, and Henry Wore His Green Sneakers* by Merle Peek. Compile the pages into a class book.

Example:
  Randy wore his tan cowboy hat all day long.

List Poem

Children use reproducible page 58 to write about a favorite adult. On the left side of the page, students fill in the information, guessing where necessary. On the right side, they write a list poem about the person. This makes a nice card or book for a special occasion like Father's Day or Mother's Day.

Fashion Statement

The Principal's New Clothes by Stephanie Calmenson is an amusing version of "The Emperor's New Clothes" that takes place in a school setting. Students write a detailed description of an original head-to-toe outfit that would help the principal do his/her job more efficiently. For example, a Superman cape might help the principal get to the playground quickly.

Grandparents Are Special

My Grandma Has Black Hair by Mary Hoffman describes a grandmother who is anything but typical. This grandma is silly, cannot cook, and has no gray hair. Students write about the unique qualities of their grandmother, grandfather, or an older relative.

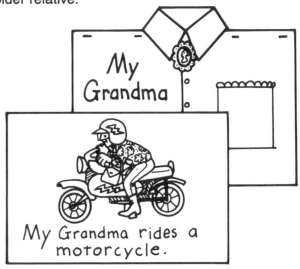

Thank-You Letters

The Shirt Book makes an excellent cover for thank-you letters to parent helpers, classroom visitors, school staff members, and so on. Students can also write a letter to their favorite teacher for Teacher Appreciation Day.

Student Autobiography

Students write an autobiography and decorate the cover to resemble their favorite outfit.

Poof Book

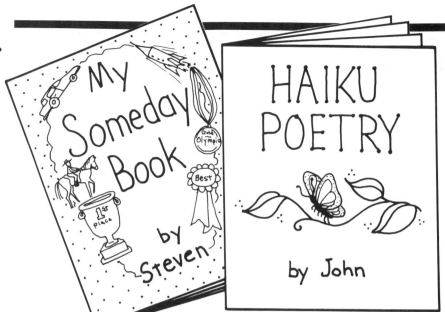

Materials

- 9" x 12" (or 12" x 18") construction paper
- scissors
- crayons, markers

Instructions for Making the Book

1. Fold the paper in half widthwise. Then fold it once more in the same direction.

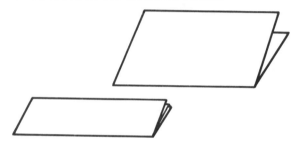

2. Fold the paper in half in the opposite direction.

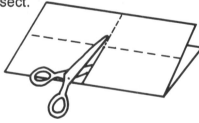

3. Open to a half sheet. Starting from the folded edge, cut along the crease. Stop where the fold lines intersect.

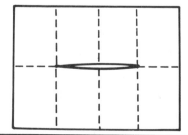

4. Open paper completely.

5. Fold paper lengthwise.

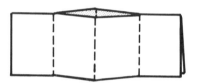

6. Grasp the outer edges as shown and push them towards the center. The opening should "poof" out. Keep pushing until a book of four sections is formed.

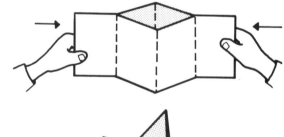

7. Fold the pages closed and write the title of the book and the author's name on the cover.

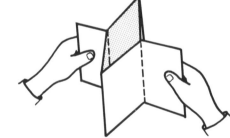

Writing Ideas for Poof Book

Quiet Time

In *Five Minutes' Peace* by Jill Murphy, Mrs. Large tries to find a few quiet moments away from her elephant children, but they follow her even into the bathtub. Students illustrate and write about what they would enjoy doing if they had five minutes' peace.

Tiny Tales

Teeny Tiny by Jill Bennett is the gently scary tale of a tiny woman who is followed home by some ghosts. Have students write a story about a teeny tiny character.

Dino Power

If the Dinosaurs Came Back by Bernard Most tells how dinosaurs could be helpful in our society. Students write and illustrate how they think the dinosaurs could be useful if they came back.

Example:
   A Brontosaurus could help librarians get books from the top shelves.

Someday

In *Someday* by Charlotte Zolotow a child fantasizes about how life might be different as an adult. Students write about and illustrate their own dreams and goals.

Example:
   Someday I will climb Mt. Everest.

Haiku

Students write and illustrate a haiku poem on each page of the Poof Book. A Japanese haiku is an unrhymed three-line poem with the following form:

Line 1 (5 syllables)   Graceful butterfly

Line 2 (7 syllables)   Floating over my garden

Line 3 (5 syllables)   Shimmering soft wings.

Land of the Free

Following a discussion of the freedoms Americans enjoy, have students write about the freedoms most meaningful to them.

Paper Bag Book

Materials

- paper lunch bag
- 3" x 5" writing paper
- stapler
- glue
- large and small construction paper scraps
- scissors
- crayons, markers

Instructions for Making the Book

1. Hold the bag with the flap toward you. Fold the open end up under the flap.

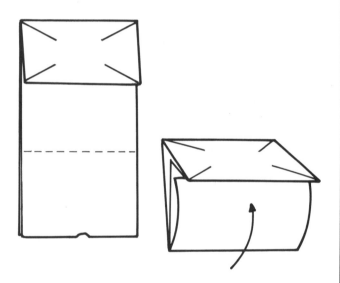

2. Open the bag and staple the completed story pages below the fold line.

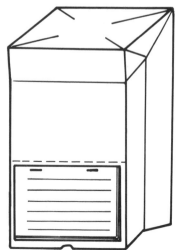

3. Draw and cut out a suitable illustration and glue it to the flap of the bag. Use construction paper scraps to add parts of the body.

4. Fold up the bottom half under the flap and write the title of the book and the author's name.

5. Variations:
   a) To use as a puppet, unfold the bottom half of the bag and put your hand inside.

   b) A class Big Book can also be made with a large grocery bag.

Writing Ideas for Paper Bag Book

Bloomin' Hard

In *Leo the Late Bloomer* by Robert Kraus, Leo's father worries because Leo cannot read, write, or draw and never speaks; but Mother knows Leo is just a late bloomer and will learn all those skills at his own pace. Students write about something that was difficult for them to learn.

When I started kindergarten, I couldn't tie my shoes.

Story Summary

Students write a summary of a story they have read and make the bag look like a character from the story. They can use the Paper Bag Book as a puppet to "sell" the story to the class.

Lunch Bunch

Students interview 5 to 10 classmates and ask them to name their favorite lunch. They record the results of each interview on a separate page of a Paper Bag Book and illustrate one lunch at the top of the bag.

Updated Fairy Tales

Student stories can be modeled after updated fairy tales like *Red Riding Hood* retold by James Marshall or *Paper Bag Princess* by Robert Munsch. Using humor and a modern setting, students retell a favorite folktale or fairy tale. The main character should be illustrated on the top of the bag.

Goldilocks and the 3 Surfers by Cathy H.

Just So Stories

The Elephant's Child by Rudyard Kipling tells how the elephant got a long nose. After hearing several other *Just So Stories,* students choose a different animal and write a story of their own.

How Rabbit Got Big Ears

Famous Person Report

Students write a report on a famous person and use the Paper Bag Book as a puppet to give an oral report. Three excellent biographies are *The Many Lives of Benjamin Franklin* by Aliki, *Elizabeth Blackwell: Pioneer Doctor* by Matthew G. Grant, and *Christopher Columbus* by Ingri and Edgar d'Aulaire.

Step Book

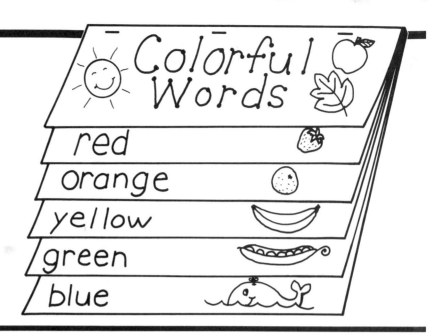

Materials

- 3 sheets of 8-1/2" x 11" paper
- ruler/pencil
- stapler
- markers, crayons
- 2 sheets of 9" x 12" construction paper (optional for cover)

Instructions for Making the Book

1. Overlap the three sheets of paper, leaving a 1" margin at the bottom of each page. You may use more sheets if you want more pages in your book.

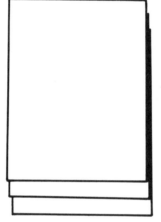

2. Hold the pages securely so they remain overlapped, and fold as shown. The book now has six pages.

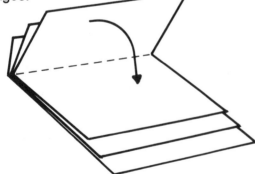

3. Staple through all layers next to the fold.

4. Write the title on the outside of the top page, or make a separate cover.

5. Write on each step and illustrate under each flap.

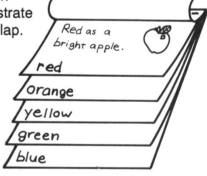

6. Variations:

a) Use sheets of 12" x 18" paper to make a larger Step Book.

b) The Step Book may also be turned sideways as shown below.

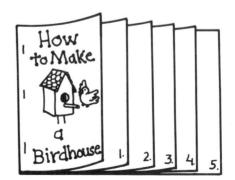

Writing Ideas for Step Book

Very Hungry Book

The Very Hungry Caterpillar by Eric Carle follows the metamorphosis of a ravenous caterpillar into a beautiful butterfly. Using the story as a model, students write their own "Very Hungry" book about a different character.

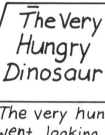

The Very Hungry Dinosaur

The very hungry dinosaur went looking for dinner.

He ate 1 Stegosaurus.

Then he crunched 2 Iguanodons.

Next he munched on 3 Pterodactyls.

He ended up with a king-size stomachache.

Important Facts

Students pick a topic they are studying in social studies or science and write the topic on the top step. Then they list five important facts about the subject and illustrate them.

Acrostic Poem

Students choose a five- or six-letter noun and follow the steps to make and illustrate an acrostic poem.

Example:

F inds me things that I like to have

R eads with me on the playground

I s always nice to me

E ats lunch with me in the cafeteria

N ot selfish with her things

D oes her homework with me

Color Poems

Share some of the color poems in *Hailstones and Halibut Bones* by Mary O'Neill. Students then make a Step Book about their favorite color. On each step they write a simile—a comparison using *like* or *as*—for the color.

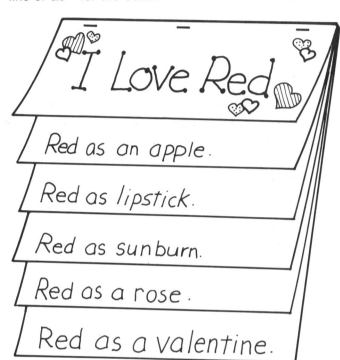

I Love Red

Red as an apple.

Red as lipstick.

Red as sunburn.

Red as a rose.

Red as a valentine.

Character Description

Students pick a book character such as Ramona Quimby in *Ramona the Pest* by Beverly Cleary and fill in the steps with sentences describing the character.

Writing Directions

A Step Book is ideal for recording sequential directions.

Making Chocolate Chip Cookies

1. Sift together flour, salt, and baking powder.

2. Cream sugar and shortening.

3. Add beaten egg and vanilla.

Fold-out Book

Materials

- reproducible pages 59 and 60 (copied on construction paper)
- scissors
- crayons, markers
- glue
- stapler
- 4" x 6" writing paper

Instructions for Making the Book

1. Color and cut out reproducible pages 59 and 60.

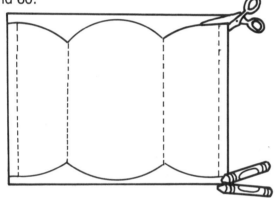

2. Glue the head and tail sections to the body section as shown.

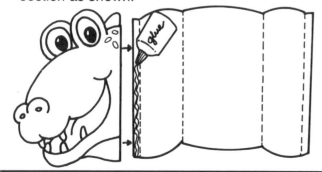

3. Staple the completed story to the center of the body section.

Once upon a time ....
A very big Dragon lived in a cave in the hills near my house.
Although he could make fire and smoke

4. Variation:

Design your own head and body sections to create an original Fold-out Book that matches the text of your story.

Writing Ideas for Fold-out Book

Pet Dragon

Students write a letter persuading their parents to let them have a dragon for a pet.

Imaginary Animals

In *The Whingdingdilly* by Bill Peet, Scamp is unhappy with his life as a dog until a witch changes him into a creature that is a combination of many animals. Students create and name their own imaginary animals. Then they write about the animals and design an appropriate head and tail for their Fold-out Book.

A Whale of a Book

Humphrey the Lost Whale by Wendy Tokuda and Richard Hall is the true story of a humpback whale that wandered into San Francisco Bay and swam 64 miles up the Sacramento River. More than 500 people and $80,000 were involved in Humphrey's rescue. Students make a whale Fold-out Book and write about Humphrey's adventure, or they write their own fictional whale-of-a-tale.

Class Field Trip

Mrs. Frizzle, the strangest teacher in school, likes her class to learn science through firsthand experiences. Read about the class's geology field trip in *The Magic School Bus: Inside the Earth* by Joanna Cole. Students write about a make-believe trip in the magic bus and decorate the cover to look like a bus.

Fairy Tale Dragon

Share with the class captivating dragon stories like *The Reluctant Dragon* by Kenneth Grahame, *Eyes of the Dragon* by Margaret Leaf, and *Saint George and the Dragon* by Margaret Hodges. Students write a fairy tale that has a dragon as a main character, beginning "Once upon a time. . . ."

Animal Research Report

Students research and write factual animal reports. Then they create an appropriate cover for the report topic.

Journal

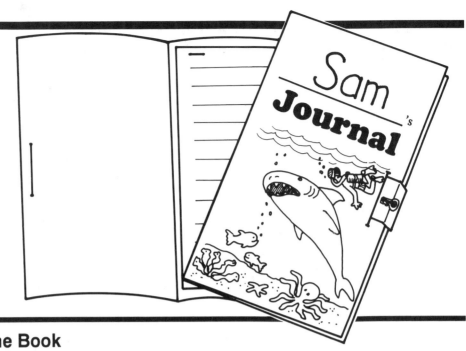

Materials

- reproducible page 61 (copied on construction paper or tagboard)
- scissors
- crayons, markers
- 4" x 8" writing paper

Instructions for Making the Book

1. Cut out reproducible page 61 on the heavy solid lines. Remember to cut the slit.

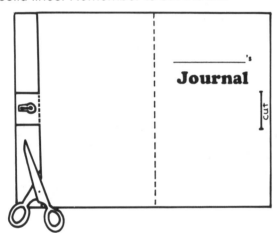

2. Fold on the dotted line.

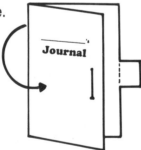

3. Personalize the cover with your name and artwork.

4. Staple writing paper to the inside of the journal on one or both sides.

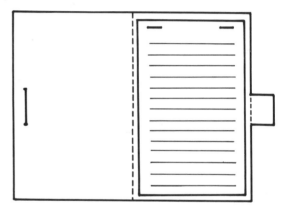

5. Slide the tab into the slit to close the journal.

Read! Write! Publish! Creative Teaching Press

Writing Ideas for Journal

Science Journal

Students keep a science journal about a developing science experiment or a class pet.

Memories

Wilfred Gordon McDonald Partridge by Mem Fox is the touching story of a boy who helps an elderly lady recall fond memories. Students can write about a special memory.

Class Journal

Compile a class journal for each week or month of the school year. Students take turns writing journal entries for each school day. Later students will enjoy reading about past classroom events.

Famous Person Journal

After reading a biography, such as ***Abraham Lincoln*** by David Adler, students pretend to be the famous person and write journal entries about daily life. For example, Abraham Lincoln might clean his stovepipe hat, work on the Gettysburg Address, read a story to his son, think about freeing the slaves.

Solving Problems

Start a class journal in which students can share their thinking about a problem or event that affects the whole class. One journal is passed from student to student, and each writes his/her thoughts on the topic. The teacher writes in the journal also.

A New Life

In ***My Prairie Year*** by Brett Harvey, nine-year-old Elenore writes a diary about her move from Maine to the Dakotas in the late 1800s. Have students imagine they must move to a new place. Then ask them to write a daily account of their first week there.

Hinge Book

Materials

- 2 pieces of 9-1/2" x 12" tagboard or posterboard
- scissors
- ruler/pencil
- heavy tape
- hole punch
- paper fasteners
- crayons, markers

Instructions for Making the Book

1. To make the front cover, cut a 1" x 12" strip (hinge) from *one* of the tagboard pieces.

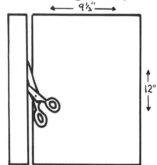

2. To make the cover lie flat when folded back, tape the strip to the piece you cut it from. Tape on the inside only, leaving a 1/8" space.

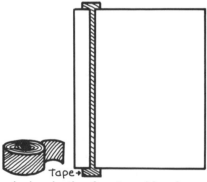

3. Make holes in the front and back covers and the story pages. Assemble the book with paper fasterners.

4. Write the book title and the author's name on the cover. Illustrate appropriately.

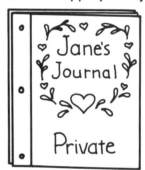

5. Variation:
Change the shape of the Hinge Book to fit the story topic.

Read! Write! Publish!

Creative Teaching Press

Writing Ideas for Hinge Book

Song Rewrite

Read John Langstaff's *Oh, A-Hunting We Will Go,* a picture book based on the traditional folk song. Students write new verses for the song using this frame: "We'll catch a _____, and put him in a _____. And then we'll let him go."

Foot Fantasy

Students draw around one of their shoes to make a pattern. Then they make a book using the pattern and this writing frame: "At first it was a foot. Then it was a _____."

At first it was a foot.

Then it was a swimming pool.

Then it was a butterfly.

Proverbs

First Things First by Betty Fraser is a good introduction to the meaning of favorite proverbs. Give each student a different proverb and have them write about or illustrate its meaning. Assemble the pages into a class proverb book.

Whose House?

Students can use the following writing frame from *A House Is a House for Me* by Mary Ann Hoberman: "A _____ is a house for a _____, but a _____ is a house for me."

A House Is a House for Me

A glove is a house for a hand, but an apartment is a house for me.

Poetry Time

Jay Williams shows that appearances can be deceiving in his book *No Such Thing as a Dragon.* Read the story to the students, stopping before they see an illustration of the dragon. Give each child two black construction paper circles to glue on their paper for the dragon's eyes. Then have them draw the rest of the dragon and write a cinquain or other type of poem about their picture.

Dragon
Huge, scaly,
Stomping, roaring, raging,
Dangerous mythical creature,
Fire-starter.

Class Book of Records

Share some entries from *The Guinness Book of World Records,* Donald McFarlan, editor. Or read *I'm Going to Be Famous* by Tom Birdseye, a novel about a boy and his friends who achieve fame by breaking some unusual records. Then have fun creating a "Class Book of Records." Students enter unique facts about themselves into the record book.

Examples:
   I have changed schools ten times.
   I was born in Spain, but I'm Korean.

Book-and-a-Half

Materials

- 9" x 12" construction paper or tagboard
- 9" x 6" construction paper or tagboard
- 9" x 6" writing paper
- scissors
- markers, crayons
- stapler

Instructions for Making the Book

1. For the back cover, draw an appropriate illustration on the 9" x 12" piece of construction paper.

2. For the front cover, repeat the bottom half of the illustration on the 9" x 6" piece of construction paper.

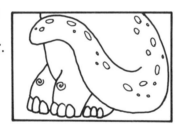

3. Staple the 9" x 6" front cover and the story pages to the back cover. Write the title and the author's name on the front.

4. Variations:

a) Cut the top of the 9" x 12" sheet into a design appropriate to the topic.

Examples: castle, barn, haunted house, village, rocket ship

b) Cut a design on the top of the 9" x 6" piece only. Cut the writing paper to fit into this space.

Examples: waves, fence, wall

Writing Ideas for Book-and-a-Half

Writing Fiction

The Forbidden Door by Marilee Heyer is the story of a child who discovers a door to the outside world and frees her people from the underground caves where they have lived for years. Students write a story about someone who lives in an unusual place—under the sea, under a toadstool, in a cave, on another planet.

I'm Scared

After hearing or reading *The Knight Who Was Afraid of the Dark* by Barbara Hazen, students design a cover that looks like a castle and write about something they fear.

By the Sea

Students make a cover with an underwater motif and write on one of the following topics: sea animals, oceanography, a whale watching trip, or an undersea treasure hunt.

Word Pictures

Students write a paragraph giving a vivid word picture of what they would see if they were floating far above the earth in a hot-air balloon.

If I Were President

Students make their cover look like the White House or Capitol and write about what they would do if they were President.

Variation:
Students design the cover in the shape of a schoolhouse and write a story titled "If I Were Principal of _____ School."

A Story Sequel

In the Newbery Medal book *Sarah, Plain and Tall* by Patricia MacLachlan, Sarah travels from the Maine seashore to a frontier farm to live with Anna, Caleb, and their widowed father. Students write a new chapter for the book, telling what happens after Papa and Sarah are married. Then they illustrate the cover with a prairie scene.

Video Book

Materials

- reproducible pages 62 and 63
- scissors
- 4" x 10" writing paper
- stapler
- glue
- crayons, markers
- 2 sheets of 9" x 12" construction paper for the cover

Instructions for Making the Book

1. Decorate the top half of reproducible page 62 and cut slits A and B.

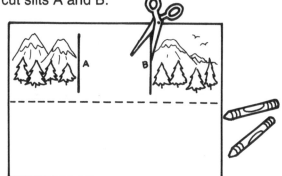

2. Write a story and staple it to the bottom half of the page as shown.

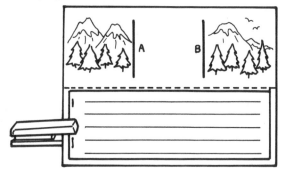

3. Cut out the video-tape strips on reproducible page 63 and glue them together. Sequentially illustrate your story in the boxes.

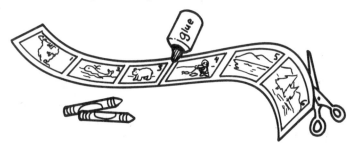

4. Starting from the back, pull the video-tape strip up through slit B and down through slit A. (For easy storage of the Video Book, fold back the strip so it does not extend beyond the page.)

5. Staple the cover at the top and write the title and the author's name on the front.

Writing Ideas for Video Book

Questions and Answers

Is Your Mama a Llama? by Deborah Guarino is a rhyming story about a baby llama who tries to find his mama but encounters many other animals instead. Following the pattern in the book, students make their own rhyming book and illustrate the animals they name.

Video Poetry

Students select a short poem from an anthology like *Ride a Purple Pelican* by Jack Prelutsky. They copy each part of the poem on a separate piece of writing paper and illustrate it on the video-tape reproducible.

Video Cartoon

Students draw a six-frame cartoon strip and practice the proper use of quotation marks by writing a dialogue on their story paper.

Co-authoring a Video

Bunnicula, the title of a humorous book by Deborah and James Howe, is a good example of a portmanteau word—a word formed by combining the sounds and meanings of two words. Students combine two animal names to make up their own portmanteau words and then write about what the new animals can do. This would be an excellent time to have an older class work with a younger group to co-author a Video Book.

Video Travelogue

Students select a state to research, then write and illustrate a report about it. This report could be written as a travelogue.

Story Summary

In *Sir Gawain and the Loathly Lady* by Selina Hastings, a knight tries to help King Arthur keep his promise to marry a horrible hag who has saved the king's life. Students illustrate six important parts of the story and write captions for them. This activity can be done with six chapters of any short novel.

Flip Book

Materials

- reproducible page 64
- scissors
- crayons, markers
- stapler

Instructions for Making the Book

1. Following the directions below, draw an animal on reproducible page 64. The body will be divided into three sections.

  A. Draw the head in section A, starting the neck at the two small dots.

  B. Draw the torso in section B, starting at the small dots and ending at the large dots.

  C. Draw the rest of the body in section C, starting at the large dots.

2. Write a sentence in the following format:

  A. In section A, name and write a description of the character.

  B. In section B, tell about the action taking place.

  C. In section C, tell where and when the action happened.

3. To make a class book, staple all the student pages together with a cover. Then cut through all the pages as shown.

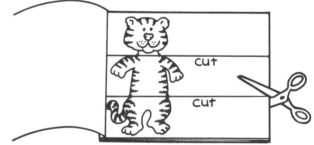

4. The reader can make humorous new pictures and stories by flipping pages at random.

Writing Ideas for Flip Book

Students use the writing format described on page 34 for the following activities:

Colorful Clowns

Students make a Flip Book of clowns with different eyes, mouths, noses, feet, and so on.

A goofy laughing clown

brought flowers for his girlfriend

under the big top.

Flipping Out Over Monsters

Where the Wild Things Are by Maurice Sendak is the story of a boy who dreams of a faraway land inhabited by wild monsters. Students make a Flip Book of monsters.

The green one-eyed monster

Slimed the Empire State Building

in the dead of night.

Fairy Tale Flips

Students make a Flip Book of fairy tale characters. *The Random House Book of Fairy Tales*, adapted by Amy Ehrlich, offers a good selection of stories.

Animal Antics

Students make a Flip Book of animals.

The green funny frog

flapped it's flipper

in the cabbage patch.

Which Witch?

Share some of the poems in *Best Witches: Poems for Halloween* by Jane Yolen or *Witch Poems,* edited by Daisy Wallace. Students make a Flip Book of witches.

Mythical Madness

After reading *d'Aulaires' Book of Greek Myths* by Ingri and Edgar d'Aulaire or *Theseus and the Minotaur* by Leonard Fisher, students make a Flip Book of mythical creatures.

The beautiful unicorn

shoots arrows of happiness

as he walks in the meadow.

Person Book

Materials

- 12" x 18" construction paper
- 6" x 6" construction paper
- scissors
- glue
- crayons, markers
- construction paper scraps
- 8" x 5" writing paper
- stapler

Instructions for Making the Book

1. Fold a piece of 12" x 18" construction paper into eight equal sections as shown.

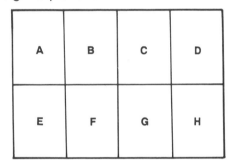

2. Cut out sections E and H. Save these for arm pieces.

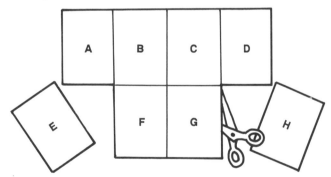

3. Fold sections A and D toward the center to make a vest or jacket. Glue on the arms as shown.

4. Cut a head from the 6" x 6" piece of construction paper. Glue it to the top of sections B and C. To make pants, cut a small triangle between sections F and G as shown.

5. Draw a face; add hair and clothing. Add hands and shoes cut from paper scraps.

6. Staple the story pages as shown.

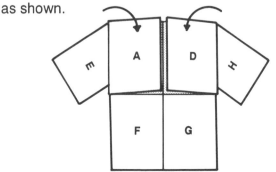

Read! Write! Publish!   Creative Teaching Press

Writing Ideas for Person Book

Friends Are Forever

After reading books about friends, like *George and Martha* by James Marshall or *Friends* by Helme Heine, students write about a friend and illustrate the Person Book to look like that friend.

Teacher for a Day

In *Miss Nelson Is Missing!* by Harry Allard, Miss Viola Swamp, a strict substitute teacher, straightens out an unruly class. Students write about what they would do to change the behavior of the class. They make the front of the Person Book look like Miss Nelson and the back like Miss Viola Swamp.

Bad Day Blues

Using *Alexander and the Terrible, Horrible, No Good, Very Bad Day* by Judith Viorst as a model, students write about an especially bad (or good) day in their lives.

Telling Jokes

A joke book like *A Very Mice Joke Book* by Karen Jo Gounaud can be the inspiration for a student-made joke book with a clown on the cover. This is a good cooperative learning activity.

Character Description

Students make a Person Book resembling a favorite book character and write a character description.

Famous Person Report

Students research famous men and women and make their Person Book look like one of them. They record their research on the story pages.

Wheel Book

Materials

- reproducible pages 65 and 66
- scissors
- glue
- crayons, markers
- paper fastener
- 9" x 12" construction paper
- 5-1/2" x 8-1/2" writing paper
- stapler

Instructions for Making the Book

1. Decide which *one* of the openings you want to use on reproducible page 65 and cut it out. Then fold the page closed on the dotted line.

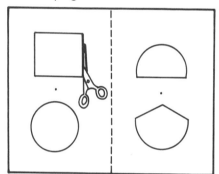

2. Cut out the wheel on reproducible page 66 and place it behind the opening. Attach the wheel with a paper fastener to the back cover only.

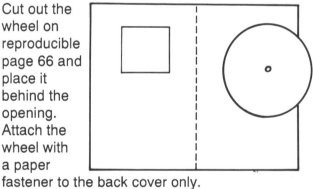

3. Glue the two corners shut.

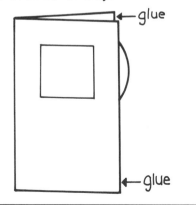

4. Draw a picture on the front cover.

5. Draw pictures on the wheel. Keep the wheel turning until you have drawn pictures all around it.

6. Glue the wheel page onto the right side of a sheet of 9" x 12" construction paper as shown. Staple the story on the left side.

7. For a class book, fasten all the student pages into a 9" x 12" cover.

Writing Ideas for Wheel Book

A Song in Action

Sing "There Was an Old Lady Who Swallowed a Fly." Students draw on the wheel all of the things the old lady swallowed, or they make up new things for her to swallow.

My Wishes

In **Barney Bipple's Magic Dandelions** by Carol Chapman, Barney's magic dandelions grant his wishes. Students write a story about a person or thing that grants their wishes and illustrate those wishes on the wheel.

Writing a Plan

In **A Garden for a Groundhog** by Lorna Balian, Mr. O'Leary tries to find a way to keep a groundhog from eating all the vegetables in his garden. Students write and illustrate a plan for keeping the groundhog from eating Mr. O'Leary's vegetables.

The groundhog thinks the garden was planted just for him.

Raining Ravioli

Cloudy With a Chance of Meatballs by Judi Barrett tells about the unusual town of Chewandswallow where all food is provided by the weather. Students write a story about a make-believe town like Chewandswallow. They give the town a name and draw on the wheel the things that fall from the sky.

Cycles in Nature

Students illustrate a natural cycle on the wheel and describe the cycle in writing.

Examples:
   the water cycle
   the life cycle of a butterfly
   the carbon cycle

Action Summary

The Wheel Book is an excellent model for students to use to summarize an episode from a novel. For a hilarious example, share the episode from **Homer Price** by Robert McCloskey that describes Homer's predicament when the doughnut machine goes out of control.

The doughnut machine goes out of control.

Accordion Book

Materials

- 12" x 36" (approx.) butcher paper
- 2 pieces of cardboard or tagboard
- colored paper for covers (optional)
- scissors
- writing paper
- glue
- crayons, markers

Instructions for Making the Book

1. Fold butcher paper in half lengthwise for strength. For a longer book, use a longer piece of butcher paper.

2. Fold the butcher paper accordion style into equal parts. The size of the resulting sections will determine what size cardboard and writing paper you will use.

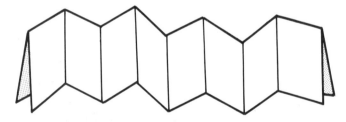

3. To make the book sturdy, glue a piece of cardboard or tagboard inside each end section as shown.

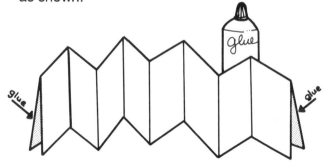

4. To make a front cover, appropriately illustrate the front section, or glue on a cover made from colored paper. Leave the last section as is or glue on a back cover.

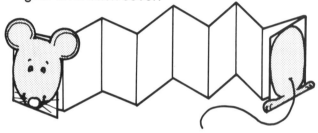

5. Glue story pages on the segments.

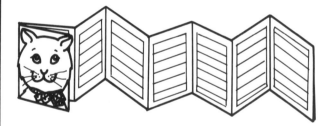

6. Variation:

Segments can be left as is or cut into different shapes.

Writing Ideas for Accordion Book

Thoroughly Thankful

Students write about what they are thankful for. They illustrate the front cover like a turkey and the back cover with feathers.

Very Special People

Students make their book look like a bear and write about "A Beary Special Person."

Insect Information

Children research scientific information about the insects in the book *The Very Quiet Cricket* by Eric Carle. They record facts about one kind of insect on the sections of the Accordion Book and illustrate the covers appropriately.

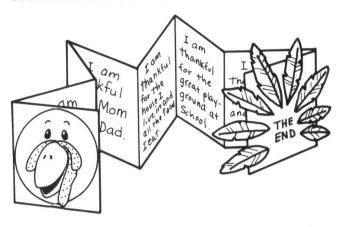

Late Again

In *John Patrick Norman McHennessy: The Boy Who Was Always Late* by John Burningham, John's teacher doubts his wild excuses for being late to school. Students write their own creative excuses for being late to school. They make the book in the shape of a school building.

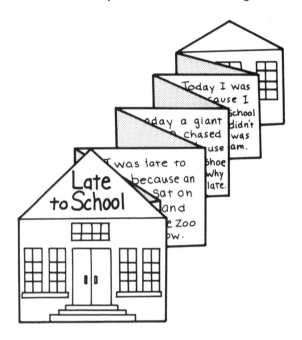

Fantastic Field Trips

Read *The Magic School Bus: Lost in the Solar System* or another book in the series by Joanna Cole. Students write about a field trip the class has taken or about a fantasy field trip and make the cover in the shape of a school bus.

VIP's

Following the pattern in *The Important Book* by Margaret Wise Brown, students write about important people in their lives. Or they can write about the important elements in a unit of study.

Examples:

> The important thing about my friend (mom, brother, grandmother) is . . .

> The important thing about democracy (a reptile, long division, Thomas Edison) is . . .

Basic Hard-Cover Book

Materials

- 2 pieces of 5" x 7" cardboard
- 10" x 13" wallpaper
- 9" x 6" tagboard
- cloth tape
- scissors
- ruler/pencil
- glue
- 8-1/2" x 5-1/2" story paper (folded widthwise)
- long-arm stapler

Instructions for Making the Book

1. Using cloth tape and leaving a 1/2" space, tape the two pieces of cardboard together in the center.

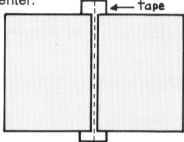

2. Center the taped cardboard pieces on the back of the wallpaper. Trace around the cardboard and draw the side and end flaps as shown.

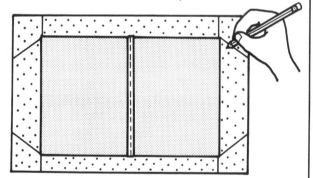

3. Trim the corners of the wallpaper as shown.

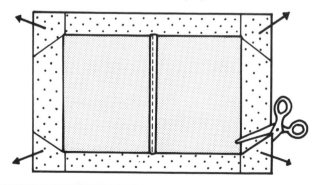

4. Spread white glue all over the back of the wallpaper. Reposition the cardboard pieces and fold up the sides and end flaps.

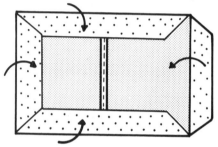

5. If the book does not close easily, cut a V-shaped piece in the wallpaper as shown.

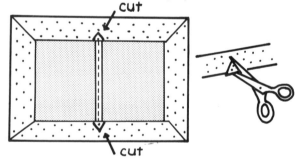

6. Fold the tagboard in half. Staple the completed story pages to the tagboard on the center fold. Glue the tagboard to the inside of the cover.

Writing Ideas for Basic Hard-Cover Book

Kind Comments

In *The Tenth Good Thing About Barney* by Judith Viorst, a young boy's parents help him deal with the death of his pet cat by asking him to think of ten good things to remember about Barney. Students write a story telling ten good things about their pet, their mom, their sister/brother, or a classmate.

Parent Power

The main characters in the companion books *When I Have a Little Boy* and *When I Have a Little Girl* by Charlotte Zolotow tell how they will raise their own children. Students write about things they will and will not allow their children to do when they become parents.

Save the Earth

In *Just a Dream* by Chris Van Allsburg a young boy visits the future, but it is not what he expects. It is an environmental disaster. Have students write a plan to conserve resources and clean up the earth.

Champions

Discuss the fact that everyone is a champion in some way. Emphasize a variety of qualities such as punctuality, kindness, academic scholarship, athletic skills, and artistic talents. Students make a list of their personal strengths. Then they pick one and write a story about this championship quality.

Journal Writing

The Basic Hard-Cover Book makes a durable journal that can be used by students on a daily basis to record thoughts, feelings, and observations.

Autobiographical Penny Pages

The Hundred Penny Box by Sharon Mathis is the touching account of a young black boy and his one-hundred-year-old great-great-aunt Dew, who tells him stories about her long life. Students find pennies minted in each year of their life and glue each one onto a separate page. With the help of a parent, they write one or more significant events for each year.

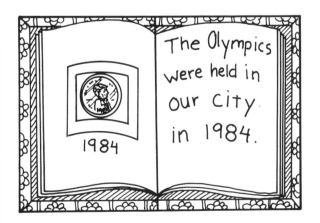

Slit Book

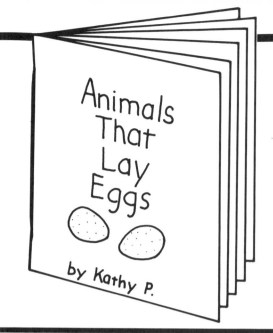

Materials

- 3 pieces of 8-1/2" x 11" unlined paper
- scissors
- ruler
- pencil

Instructions for Making the Book

1. Fold the three pieces of paper in half as shown. For longer stories, use additional pieces of paper to create the necessary number of pages.

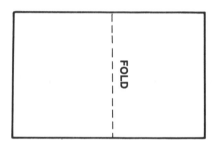

2. Open *one* of the folded sheets and bend it in half lengthwise. (Do not crease it.) Cut on the fold line from the bend to within 1" of the edge of the paper.

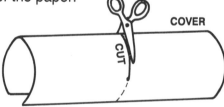

3. Take the remaining pieces of paper and cut in 1" from each edge on the fold as shown.

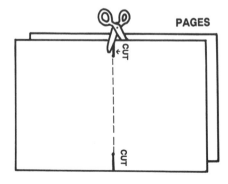

4. Bend the book pages in half lengthwise and slide them through the long slit in the cover.

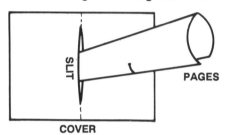

5. Ease open the pages until they fit into the slit.

I was really sad the day my hamster died.

6. Fold and you have a book.

Feelings

Writing Ideas for Slit Book

Feelings

Students make a book about their feelings, illustrating and writing about a different feeling (angry, sad, happy, excited, hurt, brave, friendly) on each page.

An Alphabet Feast

In *Alligator Arrived With Apples: A Potluck Alphabet Feast* by Crescent Dragonwagon, a menagerie of animals bring unusual foods to a Thanksgiving celebration. Students choose six or more letters of the alphabet and write and illustrate alliterative phrases about the foods the animals would bring to a party.

Animal Facts

Chickens Aren't the Only Ones by Ruth Heller is a beautifully illustrated science and nature book about the many different kinds of animals that lay eggs. Students research and write about these animals.

Homonyms

In *A Chocolate Moose for Dinner* by Fred Gwynne, humorous illustrations show how the meanings of homonyms can be confused. Students write and illustrate sentences using homonyms to show an understanding of their meanings.

Example:
    We had chocolate <u>mousse</u> for dessert.
    A <u>moose</u> is a North American mammal.

Go Togethers

Some Things Go Together by Charlotte Zolotow features couplets written about things that naturally go together; for example, "moon with night" and "sun with light." Students write rhymes and illustrate them appropriately.

How To . . .

Students use the Slit Book pages to record the steps in a sequential task.

Examples:
    How to Program a VCR
    How to Do Long Division
    How to Make a Piñata

Instant Book

Materials

- reproducible page 67
- crayons, markers
- 9" x 6" construction paper (optional)

Instructions for Making the Book

1. Fold reproducible page 67 in half on the dotted line.

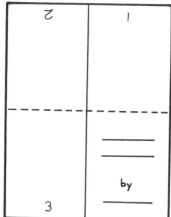

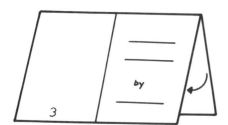

2. Fold on the solid line to form a book.

3. Write and illustrate your story on pages 1–3.

4. Write the title and author where indicated.

5. You may add a separate construction paper cover.

Read! Write! Publish!   Creative Teaching Press

Writing Ideas for Instant Book

Our Beautiful World

In **Miss Rumphius** by Barbara Cooney we learn how Alice Rumphius keeps a childhood promise to her grandfather to make the world a more beautiful place. Students write about three things they would do to make the world more beautiful.

Animal Growth

Students draw and write about the stages of growth of a frog, toad, grasshopper, or ladybug.

Fingerprint Characters

Students make fingerprint characters by pressing their fingertips onto a stamp pad or rubbing graphite from their pencils on their fingertips. Then they write a story about the fingerprint characters' adventures. Ed Emberley's **Great Thumbprint Drawing Book** is an excellent source for art ideas.

Martin Luther King, Jr.

Martin Luther King Day by Linda Lowery is an easy-to-read biography. Students write about three important events in Dr. King's life and illustrate them.

Student Inventors

Students think of a new invention. Then they write and illustrate a few sentences on each page, showing what the invention will do.

Whatif?

Shel Silverstein explores common childhood worries in his poem "Whatif" from **A Light in the Attic.** Students write "whatifs" of their own on each page.

Example:
    What if I'm not chosen?
    What if my toes get frozen?

Circle Book

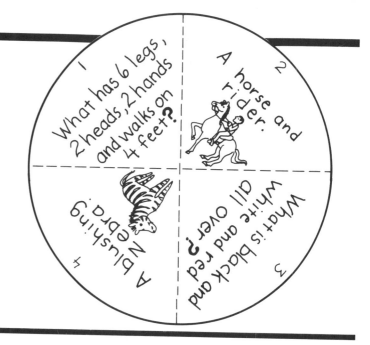

Materials

- 2 sheets of 12" x 18" construction paper
- tape
- circle pattern (11" diameter)
- pencil
- scissors
- crayons, markers

Instructions for Making the Book

1. Trace and cut out two 11" circles from construction paper. Fold the circles in fourths. For a Circle Book with more than eight pages, cut additional circles.

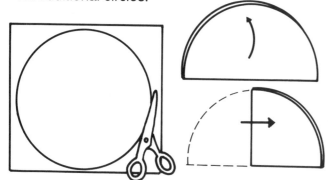

2. Unfold the circles and cut on one fold line to the center of both circles.

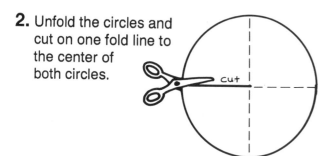

3. Starting at the slit and going clockwise, number the sections of one circle 1, 2, 3, 4. Number the sections of the other circle 5, 6, 7, 8.

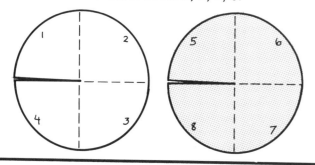

4. Lay the circle numbered 5–8 on top of the circle numbered 1–4, with the slits aligned. Tape together the straight edges of sections 4 and 5 as shown. To make this easier, fold sections 1 and 8 out of the way.

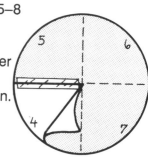

5. Fold section 8 on top of section 7. Then fold sections 8 and 7 on top of section 6, and so forth until you have a pie-shaped book.

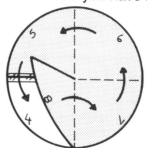

6. Trim the rounded edges of the book so they are even.

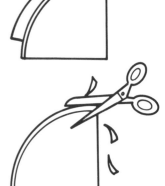

7. Write and illustrate the story on sections 1–8. Refold the sections as in step 5. Write the title and the author's name on the outside of section 1.

Writing Ideas for Circle Book

Story Rewrite

Using light blue paper and white crayons, students make a circle book patterned after *It Looked Like Spilt Milk* by Charles G. Shaw.

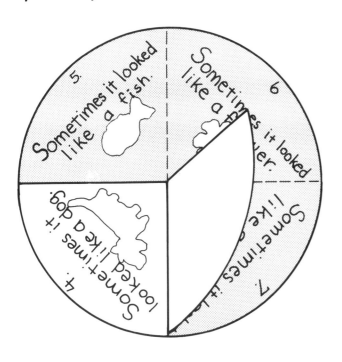

Way-out Walks

Students use the pattern in **Rosie's Walk** by Pat Hutchins to write about a turkey's walk, a goose's walk, a lion's walk, or their own walk.

Circle Stories

If You Give a Moose a Muffin by Laura Joffe Numeroff tells of the many funny consequences of giving a moose a muffin. Students choose a new main character and write their own circle stories.

Examples:
    If You Give a Monkey a Banana
    If a Cat Chases a Rat

Riddles

Students write riddles on any subject. The question is written on section 1 and the answer on section 2.

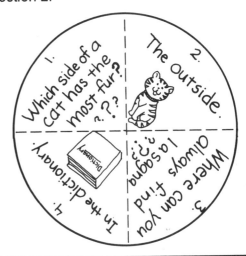

Fortunately/Unfortunately

Fortunately by Remy Charlip follows the outlandish adventures of Ned as he suffers numerous setbacks on his way from New York to a surprise party in Florida. Students follow the fortunately/unfortunately pattern and work with a partner to write their own adventures.

I'm in Charge

In the poem "If I Were in Charge of the World" by Judith Viorst from *If I Were In Charge of the World and Other Worries,* the author shares humorous ideas on how to make the world a better place. Following the pattern in the poem, students write about what they would do away with or change if they were in charge.

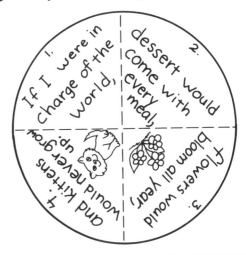

Reproducibles

Bright Idea Brainstorming

Brainstorming helps stimulate ideas before you start writing. Write the topic in the
On the lines, write all the things you can think of that relate to the topic.

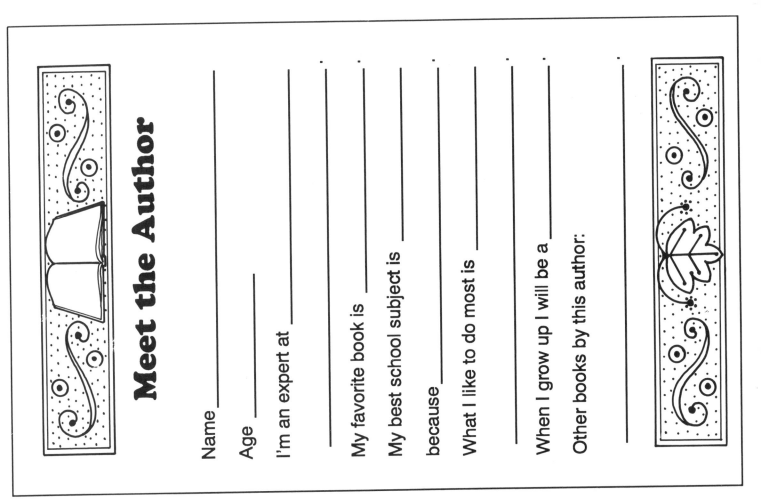

Meet the Author

Name _____

Age _____

I'm an expert at _____

My favorite book is _____

My best school subject is _____

because _____

What I like to do most is _____

When I grow up I will be a _____

Other books by this author: _____

Dedicated to

_____

_____

because _____

_____

Readers' Comments

Creative Teaching Press

Cut on heavy solid lines.

- Fold up -

Staple writing paper here.

Cut along the heavy solid line.

Fold in half and glue the sides.

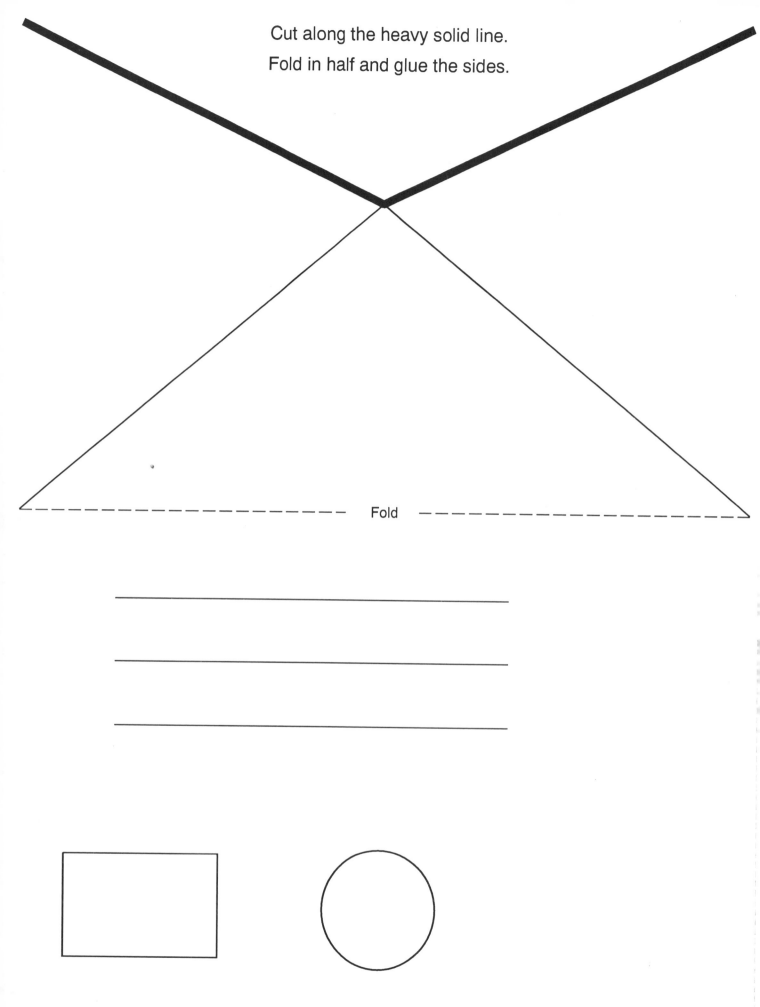

Fold

Read! Write! Publish!—Envelope Book Reproducible   Creative Teaching Press

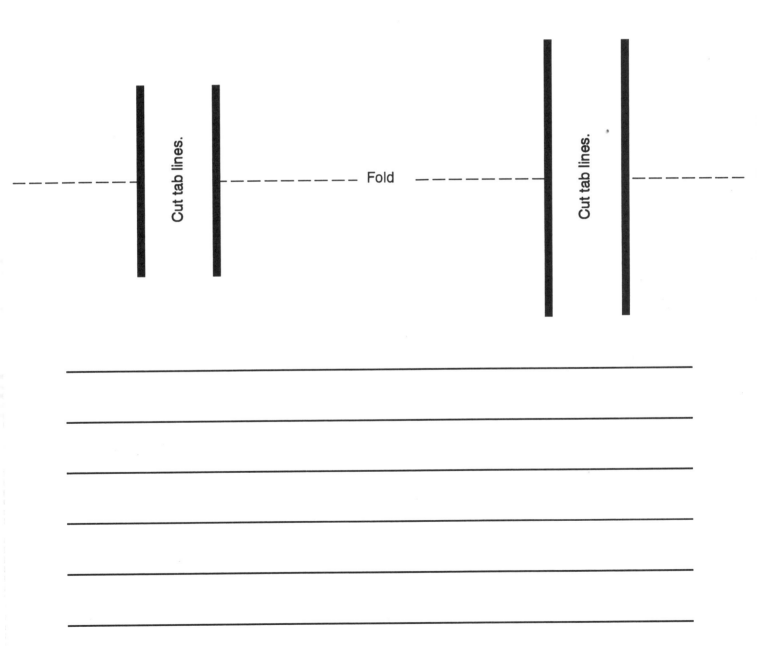

Cut tab lines.

Fold

Cut tab lines.

Name _____

(Title) _____

Age _____

Weight _____

Height _____

Hobbies and Interests _____

_____

Favorite Color _____

Favorite Food _____

Favorite Sport _____

Love, _____

Read! Write! Publish!—Shirt Book Reproducible   Creative Teaching Press

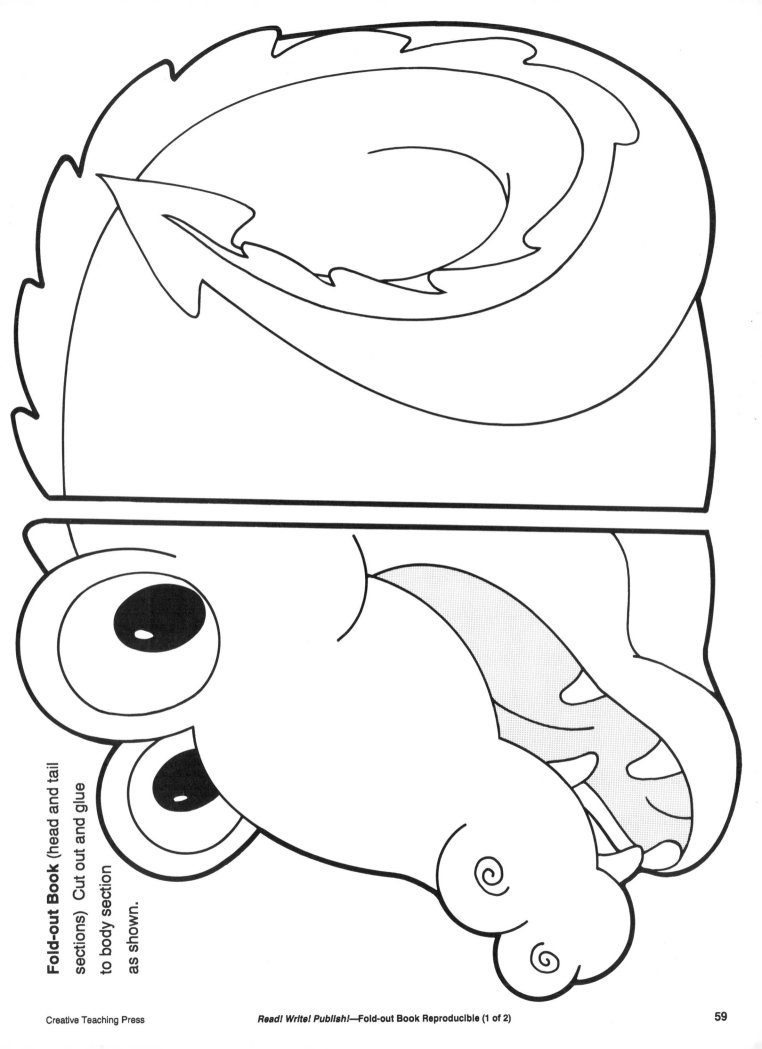

Fold-out Book (head and tail sections) Cut out and glue to body section as shown.

Glue head section here.

Fold out

Fold-out Book (body section)

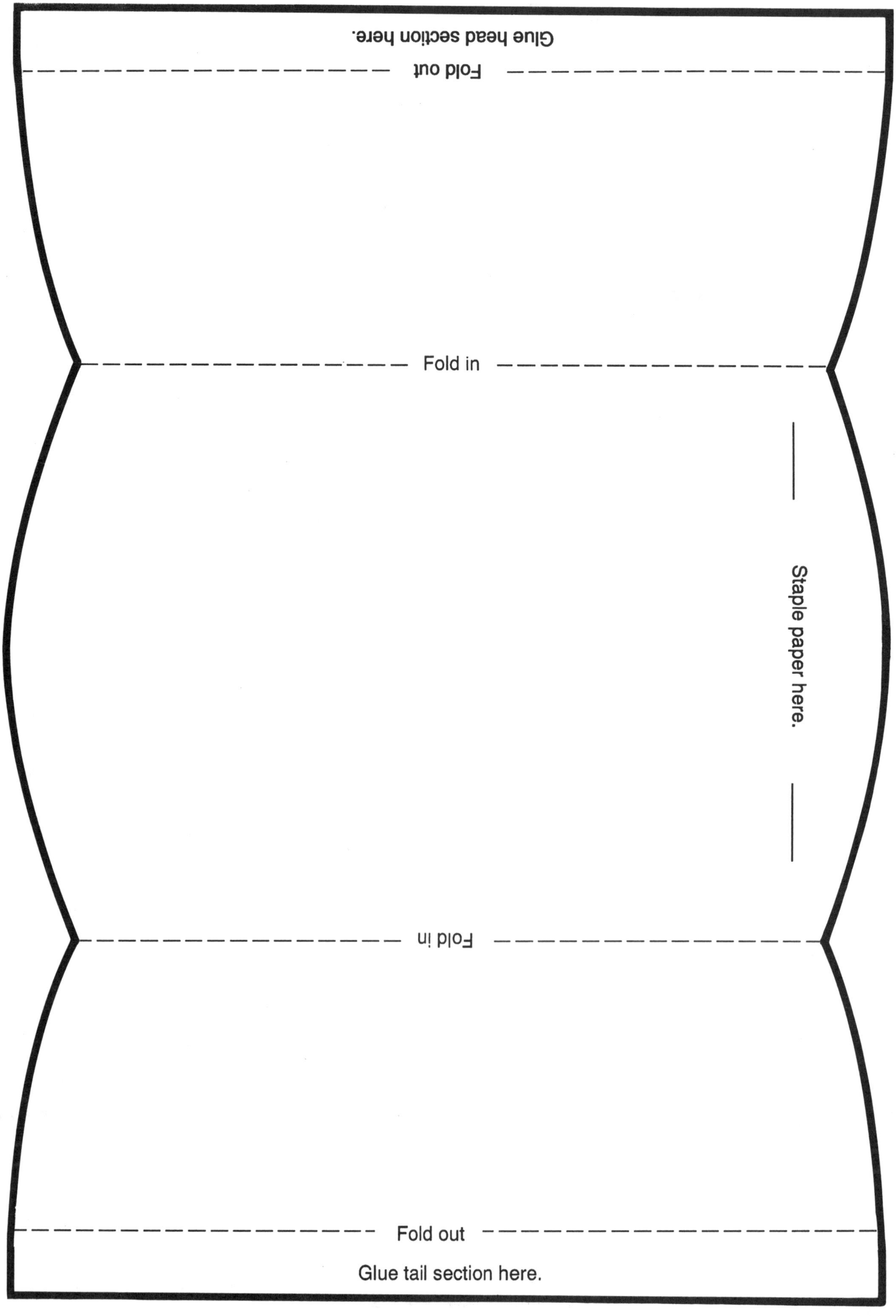

Fold in

Staple paper here.

Fold in

Fold out

Glue tail section here.

Read! Write! Publish!—Fold-out Book Reproducible (2 of 2)

Journal

's

Cut away

Cut away

—— Staple writing paper here. ——

A

Cut slits only.

B

Read! Write! Publish!—Video Book Reproducible (1 of 2) Creative Teaching Press

Video Tape

1. Cut along the heavy solid lines and glue the two strips together where indicated.

2. Draw your illustrations in the boxes.

3. Put the video tape into the video and pull it through.

Peter looked all over the garden for the way home.

Glue here.

Glue here.

Glue here.

Glue here.

Setting

Action

Name and Description

Read! Write! Publish!—Flip Book Reproducible   Creative Teaching Press

Wheel Book

Cut out <u>one</u> opening.

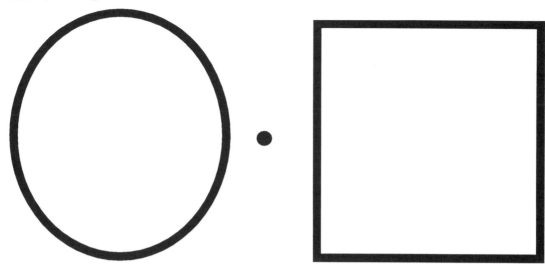

- Fold in. -

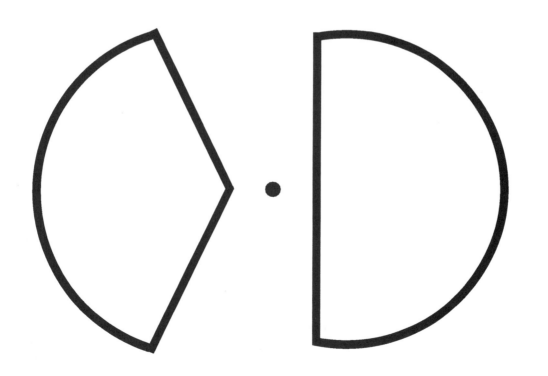

Wheel Book

Cut out the wheel. Attach it with a
paper fastener to page 65.

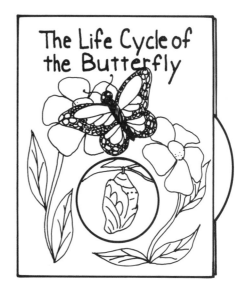

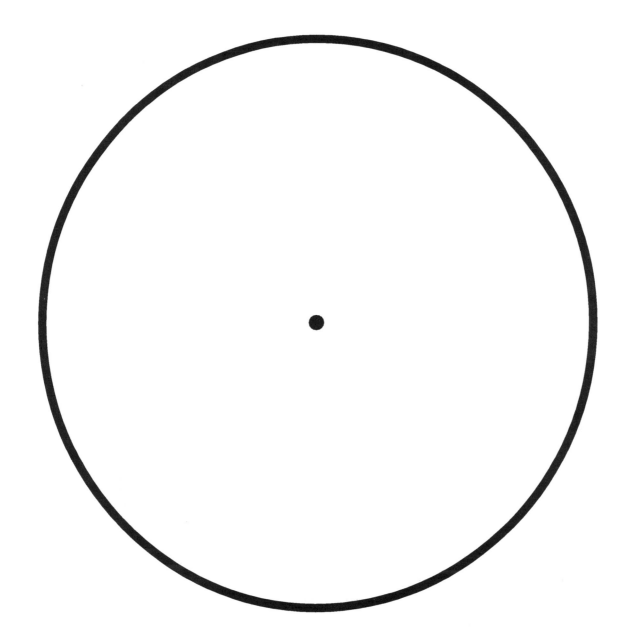

Read! Write! Publish!—**Wheel Book Reproducible (2 of 2)**   Creative Teaching Press

2

1

by
_____

3

Read! Write! Publish! – Writing Paper Reproducible

Creative Teaching Press

Bibliography

Author	Title	Publisher
Adler, David A.	*Abraham Lincoln*	Holiday House
Ahlberg, Janet and Allan	*The Jolly Postman or Other People's Letters*	Little, Brown and Company
Aliki	*The Many Lives of Benjamin Franklin*	Prentice-Hall
Allard, Harry	*Miss Nelson Is Missing!*	Houghton Mifflin
Balian, Lorna	*A Garden for a Groundhog*	Abingdon Press
Barrett, Judi	*Cloudy With a Chance of Meatballs*	Atheneum
Bennett, Jill	*Teeny Tiny*	G. P. Putnam's Sons
Birdseye, Tom	*I'm Going to Be Famous*	Holiday House
Brown, Margaret Wise	*The Important Book*	Harper & Row
Burningham, John	*John Patrick Norman McHennessy*	Crown Publishers
Calmenson, Stephanie	*The Principal's New Clothes*	Scholastic
Carle, Eric	*The Very Hungry Caterpillar*	Collins-World
Carle, Eric	*The Very Quiet Cricket*	Philomel
Chapman, Carol	*Barney Bipple's Magic Dandelions*	E. P. Dutton
Charlip, Remy	*Fortunately*	Macmillan
Cleary, Beverly	*Ramona the Pest*	Morrow Junior Books
Cole, Joanna	*The Magic School Bus: Inside the Earth*	Scholastic
Cole, Joanna	*The Magic School Bus: Lost in the Solar System*	Scholastic
Cooney, Barbara	*Miss Rumphius*	Viking Press
d'Aulaire, Ingri and Edgar	*Christopher Columbus*	Doubleday
d'Aulaire, Ingri and Edgar	*d'Aulaires' Book of Greek Myths*	Doubleday
Dorros, Arthur	*Alligator Shoes*	Dutton
Dragonwagon, Crescent	*Alligator Arrived With Apples*	Macmillan
Ehrlich, Amy	*The Random House Book of Fairy Tales*	Random House
Elting, Mary and Michael Folsom	*Q Is for Duck*	Houghton Mifflin
Emberley, Ed	*Ed Emberley's Great Thumbprint Drawing Book*	Little, Brown and Company
Fisher, Leonard	*Theseus and the Minotaur*	Holiday House
Fox, Mem	*Wilfred Gordon McDonald Partridge*	Kane Miller
Fraser, Betty	*First Things First*	Harper & Row
Freeman, Don	*Corduroy*	Viking Press
Gag, Wanda	*Millions of Cats*	Coward-McCann
Gantos, Jack	*Rotten Ralph*	Houghton Mifflin
Gounaud, Karen	*A Very Mice Joke Book*	Houghton Mifflin
Grahame, Kenneth	*The Reluctant Dragon*	Holiday House
Grant, Matthew	*Elizabeth Blackwell: Pioneer Doctor*	Childrens Press
Guarino, Deborah	*Is Your Mama a Llama?*	Scholastic
Gwynne, Fred	*A Chocolate Moose for Dinner*	Prentice-Hall
Harvey, Brett	*Cassie's Journey, Going West in the 1860s*	Holiday House
Harvey, Brett	*My Prairie Year*	Holiday House
Hastings, Selina	*Sir Gawain and the Loathly Lady*	Lothrop, Lee & Shepard
Hazen, Barbara S.	*The Knight Who Was Afraid of the Dark*	Dial Press
Heine, Helme	*Friends*	McElderry Books
Heller, Ruth	*A Cache of Jewels*	Grosset and Dunlap
Heller, Ruth	*Chickens Aren't the Only Ones*	Grosset and Dunlap
Heyer, Marilee	*The Forbidden Door*	Viking Press
Hoberman, Mary Ann	*A House Is a House for Me*	Viking Press
Hodges, Margaret	*Saint George and the Dragon*	Little, Brown and Company

Hoffman, Mary	*My Grandma Has Black Hair*	Dial Press
Howe, Deborah and James	*Bunnicula*	Avon
Hutchins, Pat	*Rosie's Walk*	Macmillan
Kellogg, Steven	*Chicken Little*	Morrow
Kipling, Rudyard	*The Elephant's Child*	Harcourt Brace Jovanovich
Kraus, Robert	*Leo the Late Bloomer*	Windmill Books
Langstaff, John	*Oh, A-Hunting We Will Go*	Atheneum
Leaf, Margaret	*Eyes of the Dragon*	Lothrop, Lee & Shepard
Lobel, Arnold	*Frog and Toad*	Harper & Row
Lowery, Linda	*Martin Luther King Day*	Scholastic
MacLachlan, Patricia	*Sarah, Plain and Tall*	Harper & Row
Marshall, James	*George and Martha*	Houghton Mifflin
Marshall, James	*Red Riding Hood*	Dial Press
Martin, Bill Jr.	*Brown Bear, Brown Bear, What Do You See?*	Henry Holt
Mathis, Sharon Bell	*The Hundred Penny Box*	Viking Press
McCloskey, Robert	*Homer Price*	Viking Press
McFarlan, Donald, et al.	*The Guinness Book of World Records*	Bantam
Most, Bernard	*If the Dinosaurs Came Back*	Harcourt Brace Jovanovich
Munsch, Robert	*Paper Bag Princess*	Annick Press
Murphy, Jill	*Five Minutes' Peace*	G. P. Putnam's Sons
Numeroff, Laura Joffe	*If You Give a Moose a Muffin*	HarperCollins
O'Neill, Mary	*Hailstones and Halibut Bones*	Doubleday and Company
Peek, Merle	*Mary Wore Her Red Dress, and Henry Wore His Green Sneakers*	Clarion
Peet, Bill	*The Whingdingdilly*	Houghton Mifflin
Prelutsky, Jack	*Ride a Purple Pelican*	Greenwillow
Rawls, Wilson	*Where the Red Fern Grows*	Bantam
Sendak, Maurice	*Where the Wild Things Are*	Harper & Row
Shaw, Charles G.	*It Looked Like Spilt Milk*	Harper & Row
Silverstein, Shel	*A Light in the Attic*	Harper & Row
Steig, William	*Doctor De Soto*	Farrar, Straus, Giroux
Steptoe, John	*The Story of Jumping Mouse*	Lothrop, Lee & Shepard
Tokuda, Wendy and Richard Hall	*Humphrey the Lost Whale*	Heian
Van Allsburg, Chris	*Just a Dream*	Houghton Mifflin
Van Allsburg, Chris	*The Polar Express*	Houghton Mifflin
Viorst, Judith	*Alexander and the Terrible, Horrible, No Good, Very Bad Day*	Atheneum
Viorst, Judith	*If I Were in Charge of the World and Other Worries*	Atheneum
Viorst, Judith	*The Tenth Good Thing About Barney*	Aladdin
Waber, Bernard	*Ira Sleeps Over*	Houghton Mifflin
Wallace, Daisy	*Witch Poems*	Holiday House
Williams, Jay	*No Such Thing as a Dragon*	Four Winds Press
Williams, Vera	*Stringbean's Trip to the Shining Sea*	Greenwillow
Winthrop, Elizabeth	*Shoes*	Harper & Row
Yolen, Jane	*Best Witches, Poems for Halloween*	G. P. Putnam's Sons
Zolotow, Charlotte	*Some Things Go Together*	Harper & Row
Zolotow, Charlotte	*Someday*	Harper & Row
Zolotow, Charlotte	*When I Have a Little Boy*	Harper & Row
Zolotow, Charlotte	*When I Have a Little Girl*	Harper & Row